BRITAIN IN OLD PHOTOGRAPHS

AROUND
MALDON

JOHN MARRIAGE

SUTTON PUBLISHING LIMITED

Sutton Publishing Limited
Phoenix Mill · Thrupp · Stroud
Gloucestershire · GL5 2BU

First published 1998

Reprinted 2006

Copyright © John Marriage, 1998

British Library Cataloguing in Publication Data
A catalogue record for this book is available from the
British Library.

ISBN 0-7509-1762-8

Typeset in 10/12 Perpetua.
Typesetting and origination by
Sutton Publishing Limited.
Printed and bound in Great Britain by
J.H. Haynes & Co. Ltd, Sparkford.

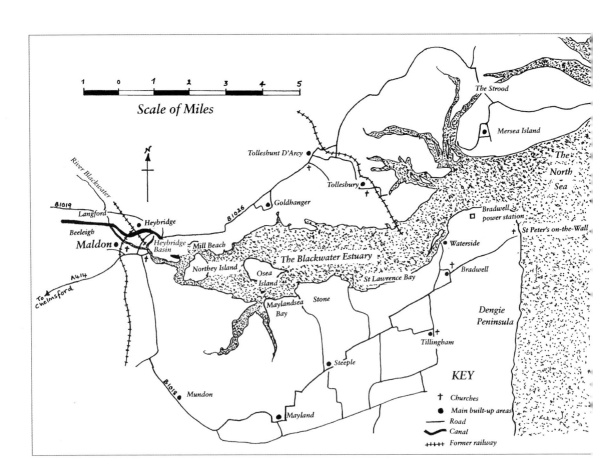

CONTENTS

INTRODUCTION

The origins of Maldon go back to Saxon times. In AD 916, a *burh*, or encampment, was established on the highest land in the vicinity, overlooking the Blackwater Estuary and centring on what is now London Road. It is now known that an earlier settlement pre-dated it. This was located on flat land nearby, north of the River Chelmer and close to what has now become Heybridge.

This previous community seems to have been a Romano-British town established between 50 BC and AD 200. Although a few fragments were found in the last century, little was discovered until 1994 when an area of pasture land was being prepared for residential development. Archaeologists were alerted when the remains of a substantial town, including traces of a large temple complex and market area, were discovered. Although for a time it was obviously very prosperous, the site was apparently abandoned in the late fifth century, probably as the result of rising water levels that turned the whole area into a marsh, which swallowed all traces. This previously unknown community was an important archaeological discovery which radically changed the perceived importance of the locality for human activity.

The town established by the Saxons enjoyed many advantages. Its site on high ground, with a steep hill leading down the head of a broad estuary, made it easy to defend, while the water could be used for transport and fishing. Its location next to the lowest point at which both the River Chelmer and the River Blackwater could be crossed made it a natural focal point. It quickly developed as a port and a market town with its own mint and a population of about a thousand.

Maldon's greatest period of economic activity was during the eighteenth century, when there was a general increase in maritime trade. At this time more than half of its population was employed in port-related activities. Many of the cargoes unloaded from brigs and other sailing vessels at The Hythe and at Fullbridge were hauled inland from the town either towards Chelmsford or Braintree and Witham. At that time an important coach route ran via London Road to both the capital and Chelmsford.

The town strongly opposed the construction of the Chelmer & Blackwater Navigation to Chelmsford in 1793 but was unsuccessful in preventing it from being built. Following its construction, much of the maritime trade destined for Chelmsford was diverted to the newly opened Heybridge Basin and floated up the canal instead of being unloaded at the Maldon quays and taken by road. However, the town retained its wharfage and port facilities for the Braintree trade for another century until the railways were developed.

Maldon continued to grow. By the beginning of the nineteenth century it had a population of 2,300. By the turn of the twentieth century it had risen to more than 5,000. Many were employed in developing industries such as E.H. Bentall & Co. Ltd at Heybridge, the Maldon Iron Works and John Sadd & Co. Ltd. Both the latter were sited near The Causeway. Bentall's was a most remarkable firm. It specialised in agricultural machinery, but its managers were also great innovators. Among their early activities was the construction of motor cars. They also experimented in the use of reinforced concrete buildings, a virtually unknown process at the time. Examples of this work can still be seen in the locality. In both world wars the firm turned to military work, their products including shell cases and aircraft parts.

Maldon's built-up area gradually advanced from the original high ground southwards towards the village of Mundon and at the same time extended to, and engulfed, Heybridge, previously a separate waterside village. A large area of low-lying land between the Chelmer and Heybridge was developed, mainly for industry, and was served by the newly constructed railway.

Despite this continuing expansion Maldon has been fortunate in retaining many of its historic buildings, particularly in High Street and Market Hill, where an attractive group of properties ascends the hill. Perhaps the most interesting structure in the town is the Moot Hall, a three-storey building distinguished by a grand portico extending over the pavement. It was built as the town hall and was the seat of most of the town's civic responsibilities. It included a police station, complete with prison cells. The council chamber was on the second floor, with courtrooms for Quarter and Petty Sessions on the first floor. It is still the offices for the present town council. Nearby is All Saints' Church. Lawrence Washington, the great-great-grandfather of George Washington, the first president of the United States, is buried in the graveyard. In 1928 a stained-glass window, presented by the citizens of Maldon, Massachusetts, and dedicated to his memory, was unveiled in the church. The American town was founded in 1649 by emigrants from the old country.

Many of the former public houses which once served both the port and the market have disappeared but a notable survivor is the Blue Boar Hotel in Silver Street. It became a hotel in the seventeenth century after being a residence for the De Vere family, from whose heraldic badge the present inn sign is derived. The building has a plain Georgian grey brick front with well-proportioned sash windows, while at the back is a fine fourteenth-century half-timbered wing and a jumble of other structures.

This 1830 print shows the busy port area next to Fullbridge, with Market Hill winding into the distance. At the public wharf a sea-going vessel is moored with a laden cart standing nearby.

In the past Maldon was of greater importance as a shopping and entertainment centre, serving the surrounding area as well as the whole of the Dengie peninsula. At the turn of the century Bentall & Sons (a branch of the same family founded the famous store at Kingston upon Thames) had a substantial general outfitters' store. The Maldon & Heybridge Co-operative Society occupied an important corner site at the junction of High Street and Market Hill while the Chelmsford firm of Luckin Smith established several branches in the area. At about the same time theatre entertainment was provided at the Hippodrome, midway down High Street, and in the late 1930s the Embassy, the town's only cinema, was built.

Ever since it was opened in 1895 Promenade Park has been the town's most popular and evolving feature and a Mecca for day trippers. It started as a small windswept recreation ground next to Marine Lake, specially created by blocking off part of the estuary, and over the years has been gradually extended by reclaiming land from the adjacent marshland. In the 1930s most of the visitors to the park came by charabanc or bicycle. Today, most visitors arrive by car.

THE RIVER BLACKWATER ESTUARY

The Blackwater Estuary is a remarkable stretch of almost land-locked salt water, with a greater water area than any of the other east coast estuaries. It runs roughly east to west from the North Sea for about 17 miles, with low-lying banks on either side. There are two substantial islands – Northey and Osea – both originally with an area of about 330 acres. However, at Northey Island the sea walls are broken and most of the island has reverted to salt marshes. Osea Island is now a farm but at the turn of the century it was developed as a temperance resort by Mr Frederick Charrington of the brewing family. During the First World War it became a naval base and was occupied by the army in the Second.

The estuary is comparatively shallow and at low tide considerable areas of mud are exposed, providing good feeding grounds for wildfowl. The wide surface water area, coupled with its limited depth, and the action of the wind and sun, leads to large-scale evaporation so that the water is saltier than the open sea. In the past this resulted in the establishment of salt pans for the collection of pure crystal salt. Sadly, only one active salt pan now survives. A deeper channel runs inland from Bradwell on the southern side of the estuary as far as Northey. In earlier times this was the limit for larger craft, hence the name of Colliers Reach. From there it shelves rapidly to dry out completely at low tide at The Hythe. Consequently only shallow-drafted craft are able to visit the town. Through the centuries there has been a steady increase in the size of ships and, because the harbour authorities have consistently failed to dredge a deeper channel, the town has faced a gradual decline as a port.

A number of villages surround the Blackwater. All have links with the estuary, being both farming and fishing communities. The largest is Tollesbury, really a small town. In addition to its fishing fleet, it was also a port for the surrounding area and at the turn of the century had its own branch line railway. Today it is a popular sailing centre. Bradwell stands at the head of the estuary and faces the North Sea. The main agricultural hamlet is attractively grouped around the parish church. Bradwell juxta Mare, a separate community, is close to the waterside. It was originally a fishing village but is now mainly given over to sailing. However, today the village is noted for two totally different buildings. One is St Peter's-on-the-Wall, a small barnlike structure, made of reused Roman bricks and tiles on the site of a Roman fort called Othono. It was established by St Cedd as a mission to Essex in AD 654 and is one of the earliest Christian buildings in England. The other building is the now ageing Bradwell Nuclear Power Station, which with its sheer bulk dominates the locality, and provides an unwelcome landmark which can be seen clearly for many miles.

CHAPTER ONE

THE TOWN

High Street, looking towards Promenade Park, flanked by elegant buildings, some of which still survive, c. 1930. Moot Hall, then the hub of municipal activities, can be seen on the left.

High Street, in the more leisurely days of horse-drawn traffic, looking towards Spital Road, at the turn of

the century. The Moot Hall's graceful portico then, as now, provides a focal point in the scene.

The High Street pictured on a summer's day with the Rose and Crown at the junction, *c.* 1960. In the distance St Peter's Church tower forms a focal point. Compare this picture with that on the opposite page (upper right), which depicts a similar scene early this century. Remarkably, there has been little change to the buildings and even the traffic is still sparse.

The lower part of Maldon High Street, *c.* 1910.

On the extreme left is Orttewell & Son, Ironmongers, where a fire started in 1892 that badly damaged properties in the High Street as far as Market Hill. Most of the properties were quickly replaced, with the mock Tudor post office following in 1909.

A view of High Street from West Square, with the road curving gently towards All Saints' Church and the Moot Hall, *c.* 1910. The tree on the left marks the site of the present police station.

Looking towards West Square from the vicinity of All Saints' Church, *c.* 1910. One of the premises was occupied by Bates, a well known bicycle dealer at the time.

The lower part of High Street looking down towards the front was characterised by buildings of a domestic style and scale, as is apparent in this view from next to the Swan public house, *c.* 1910.

On the left is a glimpse of Stonecraft, a beautiful eighteenth-century Georgian house prominently sited in High Street, early 1950s. For a number of years it was derelict and in danger of being demolished but happily was restored in the 1960s.

A view of the Moot Hall, *c*. 1960. The handsome portico is mirrored by the smaller one on the opposite side of the road marking the entrance to the King's Head Hotel.

These solidly constructed Victorian houses symbolise the age in which they were built.

Market Hill, High Street junction, *c.* 1910. The beautiful mature trees mask St Peter's Church tower and Dr Plume's library.

This attractive Victorian house in West Chase was used in the 1940s and '50s as the local headquarters of the Youth Hostel Association, where young people on limited budgets were able to stay overnight in exchange for doing a few chores.

163

"KING'S HEAD" HOTEL,
MALDON.

Private, Family, and Commercial Hotel,

Recently re-decorated throughout.   Excellent Sanitary Arrangements.

Bass's Ales, Truman's Stout, Booth's Gin.   All Wines and Spirits of the Best Quality only, at reasonable Prices.

EXCELLENT STABLING.

Dog Carts, Light Traps, and Carriages always ready.

POSTING IN ALL BRANCHES.

2   BILLIARD   ROOMS,

LARGE ROOM FOR DINNERS AND MEETINGS.

Drawing, Dining, Reading, and Smoking Rooms.
Cosy Private Dining Rooms.

Horses Jobbed. Wedding and Funeral Carriages furnished.

HOT DINNER DAILY AT 1.30.

Terms for Apartments and Board (inclusive) can be obtained on application to

Mrs. WHITE, Proprietress.

This advertisement appeared in around 1890 and gives details of the many services available at the imposing King's Head Hotel.

The King's Head Hotel is a medieval timber-framed structure which was later fashionably refronted in brick in Georgian style, *c.* 1910.

Turner's Men's Outfitters at 66 High Street proudly display samples of their menswear range, *c.* 1910.

Two views of All Saints' Church, *c*. 1890. Parts of the main structure date back to 1340. The triangular tower with its hexagonal shingled spire and three spirettes is unique in England. A further claim to fame is the fact that Lawrence Washington, the great-great-grandfather of George Washington, the first president of the United States, is buried in the churchyard. A stained-glass window donated in his memory by Maldon, Massachusetts, was unveiled in 1928.

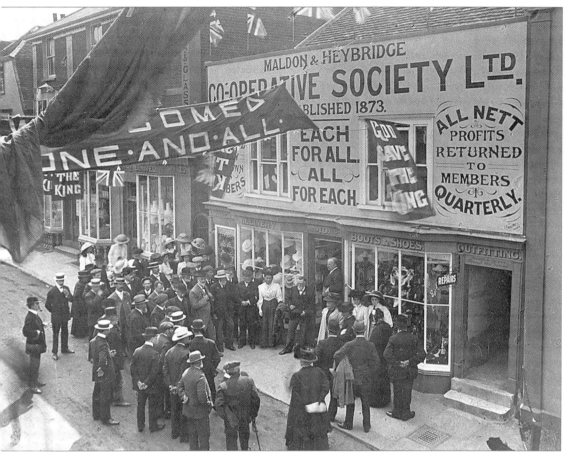

The Maldon & Heybridge Co-operative Society's shop at 19 Market Hill was the focus of a meeting outside the premises at the time of the coronation of King George V, June 1911. The purpose of the meeting is not known.

Co-op Corner, at the junction of Market Hill with High Street, *c*. 1930. These were the main premises of the Maldon & Heybridge Co-operative Society until the Colchester Society took it over in 1967.

This attractive three-storey building at 17 Market Hill was once the Maldon & Heybridge Co-operative Society's main bakery, seen here in about 1900.

The structure of these two-storeyed timber-framed shops clearly went back to medieval times. Sadly, they were demolished in the 1960s to make way for a modern supermarket of undistinguished appearance.

The High Street was brought to a halt one afternoon in the 1960s when a massive concrete lintel was craned into position at 74 High Street, eventually to become part of the supermarket now occupying the site.

The dismantling of centuries-old timber-framed buildings fronting the High Street was undertaken to make way for the present supermarket, *c.* 1960.

Maldon police station was built in around 1912 on part of an attractive garden area which once faced West Square.

Police Constable Suttling works the teletype in Maldon police station, 1975.

Police Constable Roy Crow is parked at Fullbridge and speaking on the radio telephone linked to police headquarters at Chelmsford, *c.* 1970.

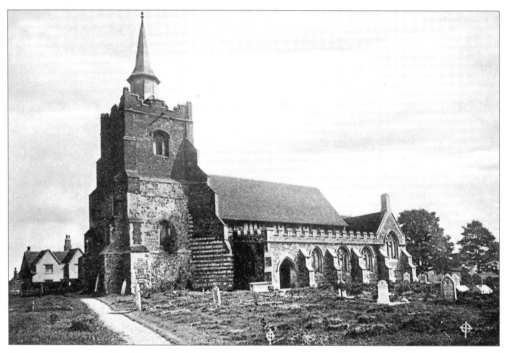

St Mary's is one of the oldest churches in Essex and was restored and enlarged in 1886 by Fred Chancellor, the Chelmsford-based architect. Among the extensive alterations, a new south aisle was built.

This property, known as The Rest, stood in the grounds of Hill House, Market Hill. It was built by Henrietta Sadd as a holiday home for young women, mostly employed in the East London factory of Bryant & May's. It was demolished in the 1980s.

To the west of the town lies the cemetery with the two chapels in front, opened in 1855. To this day it remains separated from the town by the present bypass, as, unusually, development has not expanded to engulf it. The chapels are seen here at the turn of the century.

The imposing entrance to Promenade Park, *c.* 1910. The park was opened as the town's recreation ground in June 1895. In the beginning it was a bleak and windswept open space, but it has subsequently developed into a well-landscaped park, sloping gently down to the water.

Among the well-loved features of the recreation ground was the Edwardian bandstand. It was a popular venue during the First World War when the military were stationed in the area and able to muster a band.

From small beginnings in 1895 the flower beds and other ornamental areas in the park have developed into mature features. Here holidaymakers are seen relaxing in the popular deck chairs of the time, c. 1925.

Promenade Park's most noticeable feature is Marine Lake, created in 1905 by damming a side channel and allowing a permanent sheet of water to develop. It became an instant success.

The Promenade is a later feature of the park which has been extended by stages over the years from Marine Lake towards Northey Island. The estuary is on one side and reclaimed saltings are on the other.

Two views of Marine Lake, *c.* 1910. In those days separate changing facilities for men and women were strictly enforced, with the accommodation placed well apart.

A view of the Marine Lake showing a considerably extended range of changing cubicles, 1930s. In the diving area the water was some 8 ft deep.

A view of the Bath Wall end of Marine Lake, c. 1960. Currently, it is set aside for a children's play area and boating lake.

HEYBRIDGE & MILL BEACH

Even before the First World War Mill Beach and its hotel were popular spots for holidaymakers, with visitors travelling by bicycle and bus from Chelmsford, Witham and other local towns. The pond to the left, created as a reservoir for a tide mill, eventually became a boating lake.

Heybridge Mill was sited at the head of Heybridge Creek and received its water from the Chelmer & Blackwater Navigation. It was a very attractive weatherboarded structure with a tile and slate roof. Its

working life ended in 1942, and it was demolished in 1955. The adjacent mill house still survives but its pleasant setting has been destroyed by various unsightly warehouses, and the creek stanked off.

The Jolly Sailor, *c*. 1925. The inn is well sited for thirsty mariners whether they are old salts or merely weekend sailors.

At the bar of the Jolly Sailor, six paddlers from Chelmsford are enjoying their halves, *c*. 1950. These days the pint is more in vogue. Left to right: John Self, David Eade, John Sellears, Malcolm ?, John Marriage, M. Heard.

This unusual picture taken from the estuary shows a sailing vessel entering Heybridge Basin on the rising tide, *c.* 1910.

A view of Mill Beach looking towards Heybridge Basin, *c.* 1920.

In the 1930s and '40s Mill Beach attracted large numbers of holidaymakers from nearby towns for a few hours to enjoy its amenities. The local buses successfully advertised the resort and the times of high water.

A brig locking into Heybridge Basin, *c.* 1900.

Heybridge Basin has been popular as a mooring for yachts and other sea-going pleasure craft for at least a century. A First World War ex-MTB which was lovingly converted to pleasure use by its wartime skipper is seen here in about 1935.

This engraving shows the River Blackwater downstream of Heybridge when it was still an independent port, *c*. 1800.

Heybridge Street, still with the air of a village, 1910. The brick-faced Georgian-style building in the centre was once occupied by Edward Bentall. Later, it became his company offices. In more recent times it became the popular Bembridge Hotel.

This floating container was used to import large quantities of live eels from Northern Europe in the 1950s. They were crated up on the quayside for sale in London's East End.

A party of canoeists wade through the muddy foreshore at Heybridge Basin after returning from a day's paddle on the River Blackwater, *c.* 1950. In the foreground are John Marriage (left) and Brian Horsley (right).

A variety of craft can always be seen at the Basin and here a diverse collection of commercial barges and pleasure craft are moored by the quayside, while a chartered canal barge carrying some seventy people can be glimpsed in the foreground, *c.* 1955.

The canal leading into Heybridge Basin, *c.* 1900. A few boats can be seen moored in the far distance. Today there are many more boats and the restful atmosphere of the waterway is much diluted.

CHAPTER THREE

BEELEIGH & LANGFORD

Beeleigh Abbey was founded by Premonstratensian monks in 1180 and continued to be used for worship until 1540. After the Reformation it became a family home. The east elevation, which overlooks ornamental gardens, seen here, c. 1920.

This view of Beeleigh Abbey shows the arched refectory windows and, directly above, the smaller dormitory windows, 1920s.

The entrance to the ivy-clad Chapter House, *c.* 1920.

The serene interior of the Chapter House, with its three Purbeck octagonal marble piers, which together with the ornamental ribs divide the chapter into eight bays, *c.* 1920.

The refectory also consists of eight bays with a row of middle supports of Purbeck marble, but, unlike those in the Chapter House, they are circular and the ribs of simpler design. The mantelpiece is fifteenth century.

This copy of an early engraving shows the abbey from the south in a very rural setting.

The same view of the abbey, seen at the turn of the twentieth century.

The south view of the abbey, with a glimpse of the ornamental gardens reaching to the eastern side, 1920s.

In Victorian times children were said to be frightened by this oddly shaped elm tree on the road leading to Beeleigh. The large obtrusion on one side was thought to resemble a lion's head, c. 1900.

Beeleigh Mill, unique in the county with a 13 ft fall, was originally owned by the monks. After the dissolution of the abbey, it developed into one of the largest mills in Essex. Sadly, the mill was substantially destroyed by fire in 1875 although an adjacent steam mill built in 1845 survives. The latter is currently the subject of restoration work by Essex County Council and Maldon Archaeological Group.

Beeleigh floodgates controlled the excess water from the mill race into the tidal estuary. The race was infilled in 1970 and the remains of the floodgate dismantled in 1992.

Beeleigh Weir, *c.* 1910. This is a picturesque spot where fresh water from the River Blackwater flows into the tidal estuary. It is a quiet, pretty place visited by generations of local people for picnics, swimming or fishing.

Another view of Beeleigh Weir. The long bridge carries the towpath from the Chelmer over the River Blackwater to the Heybridge Long Pond.

A bargeman's view of the canal as he passes from the Heybridge pound towards Beeleigh Lock, with the weir on the left, *c.* 1910. In times of substantial water flow, navigating across the face of the weir can be quite hazardous.

The River Blackwater at Langford is a tranquil, pretty stream meandering through wood and pasture, *c.* 1955.

Langford Mill, before its destruction by fire in 1879, was a substantial timber-framed weatherboarded structure, set immediately back from the road. It was consumed by fire on a bitterly cold clear March night, and the flames could be seen as far away as Chelmsford.

After the fire, Langford Mill was stoutly rebuilt in brick in a Victorian style. The building still survives, although now owned by the Essex & Suffolk Water Company and converted to an abstraction point. The picture shows the construction of the intake in 1924.

Although no formal public right of navigation exists on the River Blackwater, parties of canoeists from time to time paddle downstream from Kelvedon. Here a group is seen passing the waterworks grounds near Langford Bridge, c. 1955.

The beautiful ornate entrance to the Southend Waterworks at Langford, 1930. The building housed a coal-fired, steam-driven pumping station, now part of the recently established Museum of Power.

An analytical chemist at work at Langford checking water purity, *c.* 1950.

This fascinating aerial picture shows the huge reservoirs at Langford, not long after they were completed in 1929. In the foreground is the original steam-driven pumping station. The modern plant has since been built in the large wooded area to the right of the reservoirs.

Construction of the giant reservoirs at Langford was a massive undertaking using huge steam-driven cranes mounted on specially laid railway tracks and an army of navvies, *c.* 1926. The massive retaining walls were made of concrete and raised in stages via formwork.

A popular event, now discontinued, was the annual open day at Langford Waterworks, when the general public was invited to look around, *c.* 1940.

These impressive steam-driven pumps, which transferred the purified water to Southend, were located in the original waterworks. They were replaced by a new plant in the 1960s and became redundant. Today, they are part of the Museum of Power and are occasionally fired.

CHAPTER FOUR

THE TIDEWAY

Throughout history the tideway has been extensively navigated, with Maldon a strategic port serving not only its immediate hinterland but inland as far as Chelmsford and Braintree. Many of the craft using the estuary were shallow-drafted sailing barges of the type shown here.

This fascinating picture taken from St Mary's Church tower shows the estuary winding down past Northey Island, with fishing boats moored next to the Marine Lake and holidaymakers enjoying

themselves on the water's edge, 1900s. In the distance the white sails of dinghies can be spotted while
in the foreground a Thames sailing barge lays alongside the wharf.

During the early part of the present century the SS *Annie* was a familiar sight throughout the summer months, carrying passengers downstream to West Mersea and Bradwell. She is seen here moored at The Hythe awaiting a full complement in about 1910.

Another view of *Annie* fully laden and ready to depart moorings at The Promenade, *c*. 1920.

Maldon's small fleet of inshore fishing boats await the incoming tide, *c*. 1935. Sadly, the once thriving fishing industry is now apparently in terminal decline and the few remaining vessels are motorised.

For centuries sailing barges have been the mainstay of the Blackwater, bringing and taking diverse cargoes to and from the town wharves and also negotiating the many side-creeks leading to little villages such as Salcott

and Mayland. Today the surviving old boats are mostly used for pleasure and prove a dramatic sight when they are etched against the flat, marshy landscape. This fine vessel was captured on film in around 1960.

Both Osea and Northey Islands are linked to the mainland only by causeways, both of which are submerged at high tide. Here the incoming tide is seen gushing over the one to Northey Island, famous as the site of a battle in AD 991 between the Vikings, encamped on the island, with the defending Saxons assembled on the mainland. Foolishly, the Saxons agreed to withdraw to high ground nearby, where they were defeated and the town overrun.

One of the unique features of the estuary is the remains of a short canal which linked the Blackwater at Northey Island with a large farm at Mundon. It was blocked off in the 1960s by the Water Authority but, sadly, no records were retained.

A view of Osea Island as seen from the estuary, *c*. 1960. The large house on the right was originally known as Rivermere and at the turn of the century was a thriving temperance establishment.

A group of young paddlers exploring the beach at Osea Island, *c*. 1960.

Essex County Police Force (now Essex Police Authority) operates several launches which patrol the coastline. Here the MB *Alert II* passes Bradwell Power Station on a routine trip along the Blackwater and the Colne, *c.* 1970.

Possibly one of the most photographed scenes of Maldon waterside, *c.* 1910. This view depicts The Hythe, with its moored craft, together with St Mary's Church rising in the distance.

The north side of the tideway near the Fullbridge was, until recently, the main industrial and commercial area of the town, and the site of various factories, granaries, warehouses and mills, all making use of the water for transportation. Sadly, these uses have now diminished and much of the land has been redeveloped.

This sailing barge with two rowing boats as tenders makes its way downstream with little sail hoisted, *c.* 1965.

CHAPTER FIVE

THE VILLAGES

Tolleshunt D'Arcy Hall, as it appeared at the turn of the century, before various structural changes to the front were made. However, despite these alterations, the four-arched brick and stone bridge, date-marked 1585, still survives, together with the L-shaped moat.

Fish Street, Goldhanger, leads to the estuary and formerly to a wildfowl decoy pond, *c.* 1930.

The main street at Tolleshunt D'Arcy. The road is deserted except for an approaching horsebus, *c.* 1910.

This thatched cottage at Goldhanger is everyone's idea of a perfect country cottage, *c.* 1910.

Tollesbury, a village set back a little way from the estuary and surrounded by farms and saltings, has always been surprisingly urban in character. This is reflected in the names of the main streets – High Street, West Street, East Street and Church Street. At the turn of the century, when this picture was taken, the children had little to fear from passing traffic.

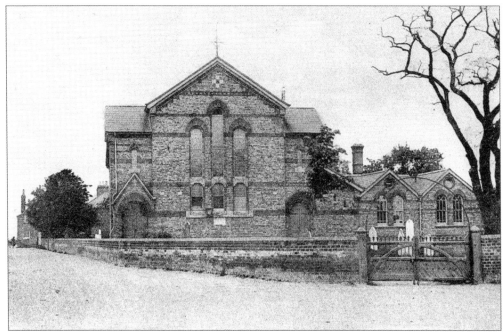

Tollesbury Congregational Chapel was built in Victorian times to cater for the spiritual needs of the villagers as well as providing education for their children in the classrooms at the rear.

St Mary's Church, Tollesbury, stands near the town square on a site possibly first occupied by the Romans. Part of the present structure dates back to the eleventh century. The flint tower, however, was heightened in brick in about 1600.

The salt marshes at Tollesbury have, for generations, been used as a laying-up area for boats. This scene was recorded in about 1910.

Woodrope Hard, *c.* 1960. On the stocks a yacht is being overhauled. At the water's edge visiting canoeists push off on the tide.

Tillingham is a village on the south side of the Blackwater, on the edge of marshes which reach inland from the North Sea. In 1910 this isolated farming community consisted of little more than South Street.

A later view of South Street, c. 1960. Still a quiet road, but it was soon to bear heavy construction traffic to Bradwell Power Station.

This attractive weatherboarded terrace, with the village shop, was, in 1910, the focal point of Tillingham. The small thirteenth-century St Nicholas' Church is nearby.

From the 1930s caravan camps became established at various places around the Blackwater and many have since become permanent. St Lawrence Bay camp was typical and catered for Londoners hoping to enjoy a cheap weekend break by the water.

Another camp was established at Maylandsea Bay in the 1930s and was popular with those who had their own sailing boat or small yacht.

Bradwell consisted merely of a pleasantly curving village street lined with attractive two-storey brick and weatherboarded shops and cottages. The graveyard wall of St Thomas' Church can just be glimpsed. The gentle pace of life is reflected in the careful positioning of the villagers by the photographer, *c.* 1900.

Bradwell Waterside, 1926. It was once a wharf for sailing barges carrying everything from corn and straw to manure, but is now mostly given over to weekend sailing.

The Green Man at Bradwell Waterside, c. 1955. This was always a welcome sight for the thirsty mariner.

Down Hall, Bradwell, an elegant country house set in extensive landscaped grounds, *c.* 1910.

Greig's Cottage, Bradwell, was typical of the many weatherboard and thatch houses in the area, *c.* 1910.

St Peter's-on-the-Wall is reputedly built on part of the site of Othono, a Roman fort guarding the entrance to the Blackwater. The present church was created in AD 654 by St Cedd, although its use for worship later lapsed and it was turned into a barn. In 1920 the church was restored and reopened for Christian worship.

The interior of St Peter's Church, c. 1925. It was once the nave of a larger church and is all that now remains of a more extensive building. The walls are made entirely of Roman bricks and tiles. It retains a simple barnlike appearance.

CHAPTER SIX

RECREATION

Carnivals have always been a popular means of raising funds for good causes and the annual Maldon Carnival is no exception. In 1918 Wm Green & Sons Ltd loaned one of their lorries to the local wartime hospital.

Every year the carnival passes down the High Street and attracts large crowds. Even today, many people visit the town especially to view the imaginative and highly individual floats. Here, the

1918 event is passing the White Horse Hotel, in those days still selling the now vanished brand of Shrimp Beer.

The 1955 carnival featured the Maldon Co-operative Society advertising its daily milk round.

The 1962 annual Chelmsford to Heybridge Basin Canoe Race attracted a big entry from many parts of Britain. Here, a two-seater approaches the finish.

The Maldon Regatta has always been a crowded annual event. Here, about 1900, watched by an enthusiastic crowd, assorted craft assemble by The Promenade.

The former Jubilee Hall in Market Hill was the venue for a variety of activities, including this fashion display organised by the Maldon Co-operative Society, *c.* 1960.

The annual Boxing Day Meet is a traditional part of Maldon life, though in recent years hunting has become very controversial. Here, horse and hounds are seen passing All Saints' Church, *c.* 1950.

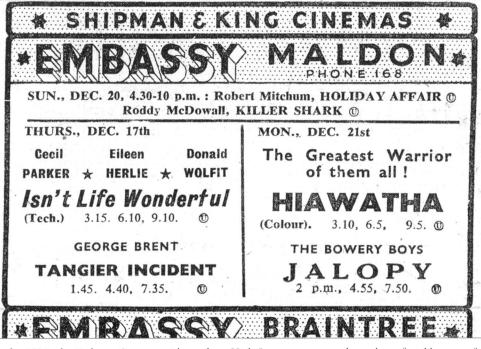

In the 1930s the Embassy Cinema, midway along High Street, was a popular and comfortable venue for picturegoers. Its programme for the week commencing 17 December 1953 is reproduced. As with so many other cinemas it closed a few years ago.

Very little camping equipment was on sale in the 1950s; tents and cooking utensils were basic and usually ex-War Department – a different picture from the sports shops of today. Near the sea wall at Heybridge Basin, campers are preparing breakfast on a Primus paraffin stove.

Father Christmas and a piebald pony, pulling a landau with a driver and footman plus sackfuls of presents, set out with gifts for the needy, c. 1920.

CHAPTER SEVEN

COMMERCE & INDUSTRY

As a port and market town Maldon supported many traditional industries such as breweries, mills, agricultural machinery and, of course, boatbuilding. Early mills were water-powered but with the invention of steam-driven roller mills many were relocated to the tideway to make use of water transport. One example was Rayleigh Mill, pictured here in about 1920.

Rayleigh Mill was established on the present site in 1894 by Samuel Garrett, a very successful miller from Woodham Walter. Rayleigh Mill used coal-fired steam power to drive the newly invented roller plant.

Coal was imported for the plant and flour exported via the estuary and the nearby railway. In 1916 the mill was purchased by William Green who came from Brantham in Suffolk. This picture is dated 1905.

This aerial view shows the extensive river frontage available for water transport, *c.* 1950. Hasler's Mill is to the left, Green's Mill, with trade mark 'Cornard Flour' is in the centre and part of Sadd's Timber Works is on the extreme right. In the top left-hand corner there is a glimpse of Maldon's ornate railway station.

Samuel Garrett must have taken great pleasure in maintaining an attractive entrance to his mill from Station Road with this rambling clematis 'Montana' and high maintenance garden, *c.* 1907.

Bentall's at Heybridge was a most remarkable industrial complex, founded in 1795 to manufacture ploughs. Later, it went on to become a major agricultural engineering firm exporting machines all over the world. At the turn of the century Bentall's turned its hand to building quality motor cars that were second to none – two of its vehicles are featured here. Sadly, the cars were not a financial success and production ceased after about 100 had been made. The firm was taken over in the early 1960s and subsequently closed.

The Maldon Co-operative Society Ltd was once a powerful retailer within the area. Here a customer buys cigarettes at its kiosk, *c.* 1960. The twentieth century has not been kind to the Co-operative movement and in November 1967 the Maldon Society was merged with the Colchester Co-operative Society.

One of the Co-operative Society's most important premises was Jubilee Hall, at the top of Market Hill, where a variety of events were held. The upper picture shows a cookery demonstration. The CWS's own trade mark 'Waveney' is strongly featured. The lower picture depicts a display of domestic furniture in 1960s style. The hall has since been demolished.

The massive bulk of Bradwell Nuclear Power Station has a dominating position at the mouth of the Blackwater and can be seen from Maldon. This picture shows it being built in 1959.

Nos 1 and 2 nuclear reactors are shown here under construction, August 1959. The huge size of the structure can be gauged by the scale of the site workers and, in the foreground, the Ferguson tractor with its trailer.

Much of the material used at Bradwell Nuclear Power Station was transported to the site by water. Here the No. 1 boiler is hauled ashore after being floated around the coast, May 1958.

A massive reactor dome being lifted into position in 1958. Each reactor has six boilers, three of which can be seen to the right of this picture.

CHAPTER EIGHT

TRANSPORT

On 2 October 1848 a railway from Maldon to Witham was completed. Initially, it was laid as a double track but later reduced to single. In 1889 a further line was built from Maldon to Wickford, thereby providing another route into Liverpool Street. The Witham line closed in 1964, the other section having already closed. The Maldon train is seen leaving Wickham Bishops, 1957.

In 1957 the contractors building Bradwell Nuclear Power Station barged much of their sea-dredged sand and gravel to the site, thereby keeping extra traffic off the nearby country lanes.

Maldon East railway station was an impressive terminus building designed in Queen Anne style with a large goods yard adjoining, together with engine sheds and warehouses. It is seen here in about 1910.

Railways were used extensively during both world wars and the Maldon lines were no exception. Sadd's and Bentall's provided much of the goods traffic.

On 15 April 1966 Maldon East railway station closed. Here a diesel locomotive is seen shunting freight within the station area. Steam trains had been withdrawn some years earlier.

Maldon railway on the last day. A diesel sets off towards Witham pulling the last freight train, over the combined level crossing and bridge at The Causeway.

In 1950 Langford and Ulting Halt was a lonely, comfortless stop surrounded by open country, with the railway track running straight as a die towards Maldon.

Diesel trains were substituted for steam in the 1950s. This two-car set was pictured at Langford and Ulting Halt in August 1958.

The former railway viaduct and bridge at Maldon, over the River Chelmer, *c.* 1912. The centre span was removed for safety reasons in the 1960s after the line closed. In the 1980s the remainder of the structure was demolished and replaced by the present Maldon bypass.

After the Wickford line was abandoned in 1953 nature rapidly engulfed the cuttings and embankments and ramblers made good use of the trackbed. This photograph was taken near Beeleigh in 1960. Maldon bypass now follows the same line.

Maldon West station in Spital Road, *c.* 1910. This was a simple structure comprising a small booking office at ground level with steps down to the platforms in the cutting beneath. After the Wickford line finally closed the building became derelict and the site obliterated when Maldon bypass was built in the 1980s. A roundabout now marks the site. However, two former railway cottages survive nearby and the old goods yard is home to a small industrial estate. Below, in 1961 the old station looked very forlorn.

In 1904 the Great Eastern Railway constructed another branch to serve the Blackwater. It left the main line at Kelvedon and ran from there to the estuary. Tollesbury was the main terminus. Trains were run as mixed freight and passengers as seen here, just prior to its closure, c. 1950.

Tollesbury line carriages were of a most unusual design. The interiors consisted of a single compartment with bench seats on either side. At each end there were open verandahs from which the passengers could view the countryside as the train puffed slowly along.

Returning holidaymakers await the Kelvedon train at Tollesbury station, *c*. 1910.

The little-used Tollesbury Pier was built in 1907 as an extension to the railway, in the hope of tapping the increasing interest in the locality as a boating and holiday resort. Among the boats known to have regularly landed passengers was the *Annie* (see pp. 58–9). The pier was used during both world wars by the army but later demolished, having become unsafe.

The bus station was built by the Chelmsford-based Eastern National Omnibus Company in the 1930s. A substantial number of services radiated from there to the surrounding marshland villages, with 'mystery' coach tours in the summer.

Maldon was the headquarters of a unique wartime bus experiment when a number of Eastern National vehicles were converted for use with gas instead of rationed petrol. The compressed gas was stored on a trailer towed behind. This picture shows three of these buses lined up on the station forecourt, c. 1940.

Osborne's is a small Tollesbury-based bus company with routes radiating to Witham, Colchester and the surrounding area. This Daimler-Willowbrook vehicle was purchased new in 1948 and used for sixteen years. Osborne's terminal at Maldon was in Victoria Road.

This Bedford-Duple bus entered service during the war years and was initially fitted with wooden slatted seats. For thirteen years it remained in service with Osborne's. It is seen here proceeding along The Causeway at Maldon, passing the railway goods yard.

In 1925 the Pride of the Marshes bus company pioneered the first regular bus timetable in the Dengie peninsula, mostly between Bradwell and Southminster, using two small Chevrolet vehicles to connect with the trains. Other services went to Maldon. Their routes were eventually taken over by Eastern National.

Green Bros' first lorry to be fitted with pneumatic tyres is seen at Rayleigh Mill, taking on a load of flour, c. 1925. Harry Green and Ernest Ward stand at the first floor loading entrances.

The Chelmer & Blackwater Navigation was constructed in 1797 to allow barge traffic between Heybridge Basin and Chelmsford, with the latter becoming an inland port. For about 180 years commercial cargoes were floated into the county town but the waterway is now used solely for recreational purposes. Here a timber barge approaches Beeleigh Lock, c. 1950.

The railway bridge over the canal which took the Witham line to Maldon East station, 1912. It was demolished in the 1980s and replaced by the present bypass bridge on exactly the same alignment.

The Long Pond near Heybridge, with Heybridge Mill on the right of the picture, *c.* 1910.

The canal viewed from Wave Bridge, looking towards the basin, with an empty barge on its way downstream, *c.* 1910. On the right is Bentall's huge warehouse, with the remains of a wharf in front.

Heybridge Basin, *c.* 1910. In the foreground is a loaded coal barge bound for Chelmsford.

Heybridge Basin, *c.* 1900. Several fishing boats are moored near the gates, together with other sailing vessels.

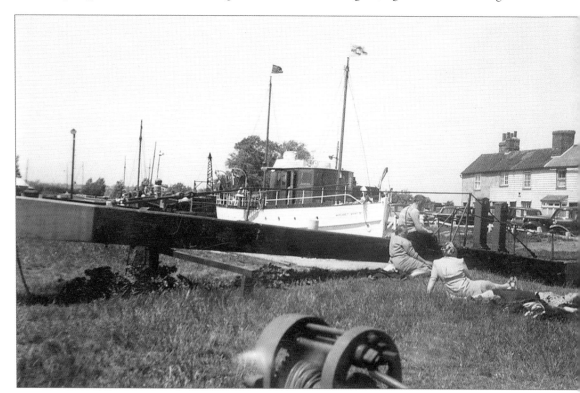

Although built in the eighteenth century to accommodate laden brigs, the sea lock is now used almost entirely by recreational craft. In this pre-war picture, an impressive motor yacht is locking through, watched by curious holidaymakers.

CHAPTER NINE

EVENTS

Large crowds gathered to witness the opening by Lord Methuen of the militia rifle range next to The Promenade, 1907. Its site is now a children's play area.

Mr Joseph Francis JP, of the Southend Water Company, turns off the steam pumps at Langford Waterworks which had become redundant, 30 October 1963. After years of disuse they now form part of the Museum of Power.

Sir George Chaplin CBE, JP, with Mr E.J. Trevett, Mayor of Southend, switching on the electric equipment at the new pumping station at Langford Waterworks on 30 October 1963. The pumps are still in use.

A state of emergency existed along the east coast in 1953 when freak conditions brought extensive flooding at low-lying places along the coast and many sea walls were holed. At Bradwell volunteers were called on to fill sandbags, which were then used to plug the breaches until such time as permanent repairs could be carried out.

During the First World War Britain endured a number of raids by German airships when London, together with places along the east coast, were attacked. On 24 September 1916, a Zeppelin crashed at Great Wigborough and the crew was arrested. This contemporary sketch shows them being led away to captivity by Special Constable Edgar Nicholas.

Edgar Nicholas and the other special constables involved in the capture of the Zeppelin crew gather outside the beerhouse at Great Wigborough.

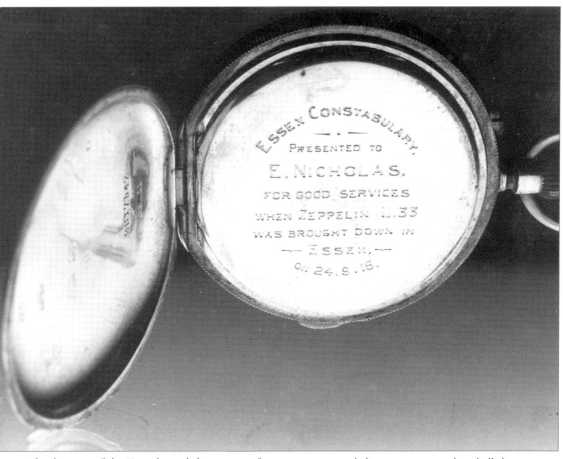

The downing of the Zeppelin and the capture of its crew was regarded as a great triumph and all those involved were seen as heroes. Constable Nicholas was presented with an engraved watch.

In April 1915 Maldon was attacked by a Zeppelin and a number of bombs were dropped on the eastern side of the town. One fell in Spital Road, destroying a builder's shed and causing other damage. The military and police were quick to arrive on the scene. Mr Bates, a member of the local militia, is seen standing guard with fixed bayonet.

In January 1963 there was a period of extreme weather and the MB *Peter Robin* was iced in at The Promenade, while on its way to Green's Mill.

As part of its 1930s programme of expansion, the Maldon Co-operative Society Ltd opened its new grocery and butchery at the junction of Cross Road and Mundon Road. The two managers lived over the premises.

The year 1975 marked a change of direction for the Chelmer & Blackwater Navigation Company. Previously entirely dependent on commercial traffic, that year they launched the purpose-built pleasure barge *Victoria* at Heybridge Basin. Since then it has carried thousands of people on trips along the canal.

On the canal bank near Heybridge members of the Maldon Angling Society compete for the first presentation of the Driberg Trophy, watched by Tom Driberg, then Member of Parliament for the constituency, 1944.

CHAPTER TEN

PEOPLE

Charlie Birch of Chelmsford Boating (now Canoe) Club enjoys a
well-brewed cup of tea while camping near the Basin during a
weekend break canoeing on the tideway, c. 1950.

In the eighteenth century Edward Bright lived at Church House. Weighing nearly 42 stone, he was reputed to be the largest man in England. In his youth he was employed as a postboy and daily rode to and from Chelmsford. He is buried in All Saints' churchyard.

An old Maldon seaman, wearing his Sunday finery, c. 1900.

Col John Cramphorn, managing director of the Chelmer & Blackwater Navigation Company (centre), Eddy Webb (left), amenity manager and Francis F. Stunt (right), company secretary, stand proudly on the foredeck of *Victoria* immediately after it was craned in at Heybridge Basin, 1975.

A rare picture of Miss Martha Keeble of the well-known Maldon sailing family, *c.* 1890. She was later to marry George Boutwell.

Martha and George Boutwell celebrated their golden wedding anniversary in the 1940s. They are seen here with family looking on outside their home at Butt Lane, Maldon.

The general committee and officials of the Maldon & Heybridge Co-operative Society Ltd gather together for this group picture, *c*. 1900. In those days the power and influence of the Co-op was rapidly increasing, with the popular 'divi' an important factor to working-class people.

A C K N O W L E D G E M E N T S

The photographs appear by kind permission of the following: Mr T. Atkinson, Mr E. Boesch, Colchester Co-operative Society Ltd, Essex Police Authority, Essex Record Office, Essex & Suffolk Water Co. Ltd, Mrs F. Fontana, Mr B. Lewis, Magnox Electric plc, Maldon Angling Society, Mr J. Meredith, Mr G.R. Mortimer, Mr A. Osborne, Mr R.A. Peachey, Mr P. Snell.

I also acknowledge with thanks the assistance given to me by my wife, Marion, who cheerfully corrected the grammatical and spelling errors and made many invaluable suggestions on the contents.

For further reading:

Hervey Benham, *Some Essex Watermills*, 1983

Peter Came, *Maldon & Heybridge in Old Picture Postcards*, 1984

R.C.J. Crawley et al., *The Years Between*, Vols 1 and 2, 1984

Patrick Lacey, *Maldon and Heybridge,* 1996

John Marriage, *Maldon & the Blackwater Estuary*, 1996

John Marriage, *Barging into Chelmsford*, 1997

Geoff Mills, *Buses from Tollesbury,* 1995

Nikolaus Pevsner, *The Buildings of England – Essex*, 1954

Norman Scarfe, *Essex*, 1975

Dennis Swindale, *Branch Lines to Maldon*, 1995

William White, *History & Gazetteer of the County of Essex*, 1848

Maldon Then and Now, 1996

Magnox Electric – A Major Nuclear Generator, 1997

BRITAIN IN OLD PHOTOGRAPHS

SUTTON'S PHOTOGRAPHIC HISTORY OF TRANSPORT